JOB HUNTING
Made Easy

Jan Bailey Mattia ■ Patty Marler

Printed on recyclable paper

D1417507

VGM Career Horizons
a division of *NTC Publishing Group*
Lincolnwood, Illinois USA

Mom and Dad

somehow you manage to roll with the changes and always come up on my side smiling
. . . know that for that i love you, and i thank you

jan

Dad

You always said
"Good, better, best
Never let it rest,
Until the good is better
and the better is best."

I'm getting closer

Mom

The example you provide has shown me
that no challenge is too great to be met.
May I someday be as strong a person as you.

I Love You Both

Patty

Library of Congress Cataloging-in-Publication Data

Mattia, Jan Bailey.
    Job hunting made easy / Jan Bailey Mattia, Patty Marler.
        p.   cm.
    ISBN 0–8442–4347–7 (pbk.)
    1. Job hunting.   I. Marler, Patty.   II. Title.
HF5382.7.M385   1996
650.14—dc20   95–525
                                               CIP

Published by VGM Career Horizons, a division of NTC Publishing Group
4255 West Touhy Avenue
Lincolnwood (Chicago), Illinois 60646–1975, U.S.A.
© 1996 by NTC Publishing Group. All rights reserved.
No part of this book may be reproduced, stored in a retrieval
system, or transmitted in any form or by any means,
electronic, mechanical, photocopying, recording or otherwise,
without the prior permission of NTC Publishing Group.
Manufactured in the United States of America.

5 6 7 8 9 0 VP 9 8 7 6 5 4 3 2 1

Contents

CHAPTER 3: THE JOB HUNT STARTS AT HOME 36

CHAPTER 4: WHAT HIDDEN JOB MARKET!? 41

Introduction

So you're looking for work...Welcome to an exciting world of possibilities and opportunities! There has never been a time when so many career options are available. And while landing your dream job might seem like an overwhelming and confusing task, it doesn't have to be. The key to reaching your employment goals lies in how you conduct your job hunt. Use the techniques outlined in *Job Hunting Made Easy* and your job search will be more rewarding than you ever imagined.

 "Ambition is the germ of achievement."

—Author Unknown

The ***Top 10 Reasons Why You Shouldn't Look for Work Today*** takes a comical look at the excuses people have for not beginning their job search. Contrast this with the ***Top 10 Reasons Why You Should Look For Work Today.***

Where to Begin starts you on the road to your job search and ***Job Hunting Tools*** describes the aids you must prepare for a successful search. ***The Job Hunt Starts at Home*** helps you organize to become an efficient and effective job hunter.

The way companies recruit employees has changed, and ***What Hidden Job Market!?*** describes where and how employers find suitable candidates. ***Cultivating Contacts*** describes how to identify and meet potential employers.

Is There Help Out There? is for people who need assistance with their job search. The chapter describes types of organizations designed to help you find work and helps you evaluate if a job offer is right for you. A Contact Counter is provided to keep track of the people you have met.

Finally, ***That Was Then . . ., This is Now . . .*** takes a look at what has changed in the world of job hunting.

So let's begin the journey of ***Job Hunting Made Easy!***

Special Features

Special features throughout the book will help you pick out key points and apply your new knowledge.

 Notes clarify text with concise explanations.

 Helpful Hints make you stand out in the crowd of jobseekers.

 Blues Busters suggest things to do that will give you a boost on days when you're feeling low.

 Quotes from the Real World describe how real people found and secured employment.

 Special Thoughts provide inspiration and motivation.

Let's begin the journey . . . Destination: Employment.

Top 10 Reasons Why You Shouldn't Look for Work Today

1. You've misplaced your lucky rabbit's foot key chain and can't start till you find it.

2. The cable guy is coming sometime between 9 and 4 and you don't want to miss the hookup.

3. Your mother-in-law is coming to visit and since you'll need to be out every day when she is here you should take a break today.

4. It's raining or snowing.

5. You looked yesterday. That's good enough for this week.

6. The gerbil died and you have to prepare the funeral.

7. It's a holiday somewhere in the world today and you wouldn't want to offend anyone.

8. You were up late last night watching a Partridge Family Rerun Marathon.

9. Your horoscope said you should avoid any contact with people in positions of authority today.

10. It's a full moon.

Top 10 Reasons Why You Should Look for Work Today

There aren't ten—you need a job!

Chapter 1

Where to Begin

You're looking for work. Now where do you begin? Should you open the newspaper and see what's available or do you call your previous employer and beg for your old job back? How will you get to know employers who need your skills and where do you go to get your resume done? Job searching can be confusing, but once you organize yourself and get started things will fall into place and won't be as scary as you first thought.

Let's start and look at what to do, how to do it, and where to do it. Let's begin your job hunt!

"Live your life, don't just spend it."

—Helen Keller

When to Start

The time to start your job search will depend on your situation. Do you have enough money saved to go bushwhacking in the jungles of South America or do you need find a job so you can have milk on your cereal tomorrow? Each person's situation is unique, so you will have your own timeline.

Take a critical look at your situation. How long do you have to look for work? Do you have adequate funds to sustain you for a while or do you have to locate work now? The amount of time you have to look for work will greatly influence how you go about your job search.

"A clerk position was available in the company where a friend worked. He was aware that I was looking for a job and recommended me to his boss. The employer called me in for an interview and hired me on the spot."

—Janet Marler, payroll clerk

For most people there are three stages to go through before committing to anything.

1. The excuses stage, in which you make excuses and don't do things because deep down you aren't really sure if you can do it.

2. The quitting stage, when you simply give up for whatever reason you can rationalize.

3. The do-it stage. You realize you just have to get out and go for it.

 A good way to make a commitment is to tell other people what your goals are. It tends to keep us working hard when people are continually asking about our progress.

Everyone is different, of course, and some people may whiz right to the do-it stage. Unfortunately, if you are unhappy about having to look for work it may take a little effort to get to stage three.

How do you speed up the process? Think of your job search as an exciting challenge and a great way to meet lots of interesting new people! This will help you to keep talking to new people and will help you keep a positive attitude.

Once you decide to begin looking, start right then. The feature presentation on the movie channel can wait until after you have found work.

What Am I Looking For?

The next question you must ask yourself is what sort of work are you looking for? This may seem straightforward, but sometimes it's not easy to answer.

You may have recently finished a job and feel that because you were a loan officer, you will be a loan officer again. Or you graduated from college set on becoming a business administrator. You may even currently be employed and feel this question is an easy one. You are a carpenter, you will always be one. But take a good look at this.

 Roll the coins in your piggy bank. You may be amazed at how much money you have saved.

We often limit our options because of what we have been trained to do, what we have done in the past, or what we are currently doing. The shoe salesperson who likes selling shoes but is tired of the smell of dirty socks may not have thought about becoming a distributor and selling shoes to retailers. It is often hard to see options when we aren't looking for them.

 "People who believe they have no choices also believe that whatever happens isn't their fault."

—Bonnie Cornell and Judy Hauserman

Few people make radical career changes but, through choice or by necessity, many people find themselves in related fields which had never seemed to be an option. It is important to take the time and look at what is available to you.

It helps to think of the people you had contact with when you were working. If what they did interests you, it may be your next career.

The key is to identify jobs which are related to the work you do.

Example

You are a carpenter. Many occupations are available to you without further training and which you already have knowledge about.
    You might:

- continue doing the same work—that is, be a carpenter.

- sell carpentry supplies.

- become a consultant advising customers on products and merchandise.

- start your own carpentry business and do contract work.

- design and manufacture specialty cabinets.

- become a carpentry union coordinator.

- work as a supply person, purchasing and distributing supplies for your company.

Take a good look at *your* line of work and identify the possibilities you have.

Identify the jobs related to your field and you may find a whole new world is open to you.

Is The Time Right To Be A Rainmaker?

Now that you have an idea of the type of work you are looking for, what does the market look like? Seeking a position as a "rainmaker" may not be a good idea if your hometown is experiencing floods.

"The studious and good never think it unworthy of them to change their opinion."

—Dr. William Harvey

You probably have an idea of what the overall job market is like, but remember that when the need for new home construction is on the decline, the need for old home renovations may be on the increase. Each occupation is in demand at different times.

Read the business section of the newspaper to keep on top of changes in the job market. The more informed you are about current events, the better.

Check with your local employment center and labor market library to find out about the job situation for occupations you are interested in. Call companies that currently employ people like you and ask them if their business is expanding or downsizing.

Locate information

- projecting the job outlook for the next five years.

- detailing if there has been recent expansion or reduction in the industry.

- outlining whether the job situation is different in various cities throughout the country.

- assessing how many people have recently graduated in your field. If two hundred people are applying for the lone welding position, your chances of getting the job are less than if there are only five graduates and four positions.

Most manpower centers create a yearly or bi-yearly career outlook publication. These list which occupations are increasing productivity and which ones are downsizing. If they do not have such a publication, ask where you can find one.

This information will help you decide which lines of work to consider, but remember, don't close any doors even if the outlook isn't great. Even though the job prospects for stone throwers may not look so good, you may be the perfect candidate for the one job that is available.

"I needed a job and wanted to work in a restaurant. I walked into one cafe and asked to speak to the manager. I told of ideas I had on how to add to their business. The manager asked if I had any experience and I said no. They hired me on a trial basis and over time, I ended up being a supervisor."

—Yvonne Earley, supervisor

Once you know what you are looking for, it's time to begin looking. Have fun!

Chapter 2

Job Hunting Tools

You know what you're looking for, you're ready to begin, so all you need to do is step out the door and get started, right?

Wrong!

Before you go anywhere, you need tools for the job search trade. A vacuum salesperson needs a demo vacuum to show people, and you need job hunting tools to make your job search successful.

"You are the cause, not the effect."

—Dr. Robert Anthony

Me, Myself and I!

You are the most important tool in your job search. It's your skills, your talents and your special characteristics that will get the job. You must be able to accurately and completely identify what you have to offer employers. You must know who you are.

What Do I Have to Offer?

Identify all the skills you possess.

How?

1. The obvious place to start is with what you've already done. Begin by reviewing your work history, past job descriptions, and performance evaluations. Special projects or temporary assignments are often forgotten and job responsibilities may have been so routine you forgot how important they were. Valuable experience is often gained through routine or temporary projects.

 The details of what we have done in past jobs are often blurred with time. Write down the responsibilities you have had to remind you of how much you have done.

2. Take a look at your education, including any courses and workshops you have taken. Dates and course content should be reviewed to remind you of the things you will want to emphasize to employers.

 Go for a walk, jog or bike ride. The fresh air and exercise will rejuvenate you.

3. Finally, those hours you've spent coordinating your child's swim club competition are going to benefit you. Outline all the volunteer work you have done, everything from distributing food baskets to being a member of your community watch program. This will help you identify those skills which have not been used in paying jobs.

 "You get treated in life the way you train people to treat you."

—Dr. Robert Anthony

4. Take a good look at your personal characteristics. Skills and qualifications are necessary, but personal attributes are just as important to employers. The most common reasons for firing employees is not incompetence, but the inability to get along with other employees or being late or "sick" too often. It is up to you to identify which skills make you a good employee along with which skills make you a good computer programmer or sales clerk.

 Ask a close friend to help identify your personal characteristics. It may be hard for you to say what you are good at, but your friend will have an easier time identifying your strong personal qualities.

 # Selling My Skills

Identifying your skills is only the first step. Being able to tell an employer you possess certain traits and qualifications is important, but you also need to be able to convince them. Christopher Columbus told people the world was round, but until he landed in the New World no one believed him. Similarly, simply saying you are enthusiastic and hardworking is not enough.

How?

- Use your voice! Sound interested and enthusiastic, not like a computer-simulated recording. This is especially important when talking to people on the telephone. You must rely on your voice to "say everything."

Speaking in a monotone puts people to sleep, while varying your tone gets them involved and makes you more interesting and believable . . . and more likely to land an interview.

- Use your face! Look directly at people when talking to them, but do not stare. Maintaining eye contact is not only good manners, it tells people you are interested in what they have to say. Look away too frequently and you lose credibility.

- Smiling makes you easier to approach and people would rather be around a happy person than a sad, angry or frustrated person. You must remember to smile when speaking on the telephone as well. It's easier to say positive things and sound self assured when smiling.

Call a friend and speak to them when you are smiling and when you are frowning. Ask if they can tell the difference.

- Use your whole body! This does not mean wearing revealing clothing or making suggestive gestures. It means portraying a positive and self-assured image. You appear more confident when you have good posture and keep your head up than when you slouch and droop. Employers want people who are confident in themselves and their skills, not someone who appears as if they will break down at the first sign of conflict or challenge.

Videotape yourself describing your skills. Are you interesting enough to keep an employer's attention or should you add some spice to your presentation?

Practice telling yourself and everyone who will listen what you have to offer and soon you will be able to convince employers that you are the best person for the job.

esume

A job seeker without a resume is like a photographer without a camera. Without this essential tool you will get very little accomplished.

Why Do I Need a Resume?

Most employers request that resumes be submitted by interested candidates, and few agencies give out application forms. If you do not have a resume which describes your skills convincingly, you may be cutting yourself off from being considered for positions you are qualified to fill. Be sure your resume is an accurate reflection of your skills, detailing all you have to offer employers.

"When in doubt, tell the truth."

—Mark Twain

Your resume must be prepared *before* you begin looking for work. There is nothing more frustrating than meeting a great contact who wants your resume that afternoon and realizing yours is out-of-date and needs to be redone.

Be sure it is up-to-date and accurately reflects the skills you would use in the work you are pursuing. Don't assume your old resume is good enough.

"Your past is always going to be the way it was. Stop trying to change it."

—Dr. Robert Anthony

Why?

1. You may have been focusing on a different line of work when you developed you last resume. Perhaps you were applying for school counseling positions and now you are applying for teaching positions. If you use the old resume, important skills might be overlooked and less important ones highlighted. With 200 competing applications, a potential employer is not going to assume you have the necessary skills. You must tell them.

QRW

"I put in an application with the company I wanted to work for and kept phoning to see if a job had become available. Within two months the owner called, interviewed me, and I was hired."

Lill Armstrong, stenographer

2. Your employment history may need updating. Most likely your resume has not been used since you last looked for work. The job title and skills used in your most recent job may not be outlined. You want to highlight all of your skills and experiences.

It is important to have an updated resume which accurately reflects what you can offer potential employers.

What Goes In A Resume?

It will take several hours to plan and assemble a great resume, but it will be worth the time and effort. A resume which accurately outlines your skills and experience, is organized and easy to read, and is eye-catching is more likely to be read than one which is hastily typed up at the last minute. A sloppy resume often leaves out valuable information and is not likely to impress employers.

Listen to music you really like. Relax and enjoy the rhythm.

How?

Sit down and think about the type of work you are looking for.

- What skills are required?

- What education and training is needed?

- What personal characteristics are useful for this position?

Write down all the skills, experiences, qualifications, and personal characteristics you possess which make you the perfect candidate for this line of work.

Include your work history, education, relevant skills, and any other relevant information in your resume. Be sure it is accurate and complete.

For sample resumes and an easy-to-follow method of creating informative, unique, and effective resumes, see *Resumes Made Easy.*

Don't be afraid to be creative with your resume. Employers see hundreds of resumes for each job posting. Those that stand out and look interesting are more likely to be read.

Your resume is a tool to help you find work. The better the tool, the better you will be able to do your job of seeking employment.

Introductory letters

Submitting resumes for posted job openings is a good idea, but it is also necessary to make contact with companies before they advertise a position. Get your foot in the door before a job becomes available and you are more likely to be remembered by employers when they need to hire someone.

One way to introduce yourself to employers is with an introductory letter. Introductory letters are used as personal biographies to help an employer get to know you better. A clear, concise letter which highlights your strengths and introduces you to a potential employer is an effective way of making contact.

"When you get right down to the root of the meaning of the word "succeed," you find that it simply means to follow through."

—F.W. Nichol

Example

Percy Jackson is an editor for a local newspaper who wants to move on and work for a larger company. She knows that when editor positions become available in larger centers, over one hundred resumes are usually submitted, so something must be done to "beat the rush" and allow employers to get to know her.

Although introductory letters are a new concept to her, Percy writes a brief descriptive letter stating her experience and strongest personal qualities and conveying her enthusiasm and love for her work. Having no prior experience with introductory letters, Percy decides to mail them to only four employers. She follows up by calling the chief editors and also makes cold calls to four employers she did not send letters to.

Three of the editors who received the letter remembered Percy's name. All four agreed to meet with her. When Percy spoke with the editors who had not received letters it took significantly more work to convince them to meet with her and one employer flatly refused.

Percy's foot was in the door with seven out of eight employers, but it had taken more effort to convince the cold-call employers to see her than the employers who had received the letter prior to her call.

"The difference between the impossible and the possible lies in a person's determination."

—Tommy Lasorda

What Do I Say?

1. Your letter must have information which is of interest to an employer. Identify the skills, experiences, and personal characteristics you think the employer is most interested in.

Jot down your strongest skills and attributes before you begin composing your letter so you do not forget to mention them.

2. When writing an introductory letter, imagine you are writing to someone you know. This will help you write a letter that sounds personal. You want to avoid creating the impersonal stuffy feeling employers often get when reading resumes. Remember, you want the employer to get a feel for who you are. Your resume tells *what* you do; your introductory letter tells *who* you are and *how* you approach things.

Have someone help you by writing down what you dictate. Speak as if you are having a conversation with a friend. You will come across more like yourself than if you try writing a formal letter.

A sense of humor and casual nature in your writing is good but be careful not to sound frivolous or scattered. Be personal, but remember you and the employer are not best buddies.

3. Your letter must grab the employer's attention without being too long. Keep it to under one page. It is better to have four sentences which say a lot than to have a whole page which rambles.

Dictate without revising until you are done. Once you have completed the letter, go back and edit. This will make your letter flow better.

4. Review your letter thoroughly. Be sure that your most impressive skills and qualities are outlined, and that the letter sounds like you. Proofread your letter carefully, checking for spelling errors, correct punctuation, and proper grammar.

5. Have someone read the letter and give their honest opinion. If they don't find it informative and interesting, will an employer?

Although it is good to have someone help you, do not have them
write the letter for you. It will sound
like them and your personality will
not come through.

6. Place your name and telephone number prominently on the letter. It is a good idea to put your name in several locations so employers will remember it.

    Many potential locations exist. You can put your name:

    - at the top of the page with your address and telephone number.

    - introducing yourself at the beginning of the letter.

    - at the bottom with your signature.

    - at the bottom as a footer.

    - along the side of the page.

Put your name in your letter no more
than three times. Although it is
important to remind the employer
of who you are, you don't want
your name to be the only thing in
the letter.

7. Address the letter to a specific person. You want the person hiring to get to know you and become an acquaintance of sorts. How personal is it when you start your letter, Dear Human Resources Manager? You must know the name and title of the person you are sending it to.

8. Complete the final copy on a computer or typewriter. Handwriting is often hard to read and might not even be read. You can also create a letter that looks interesting as well as informs when you use a computer.

Don't be afraid to be unique and try new things. A letter which is interesting and eye-catching is more likely to be read.

Personalized Letters

When you write letters to three friends you may have the same core information, but you add, delete, and change information depending upon who you are writing to. Similarly, each employer is looking for something different, so it is important you create a new letter for each.

Outline the skills and attributes an employer is looking for. This is the best way for them to get to know what makes you good for their company.

Sample Introductory Letters

On the following pages you will find sample introductory letters. Each letter contains valuable information for employers, but is also designed to be attractive and engage the employers interest. Don't forget this when designing your letters.

Call a friend and get together for coffee. Relax and talk about things you enjoy.

Dear Mark Ford,

I would like to introduce myself to you as an up-and-coming Artist Manager. I have been working in Los Angeles managing various groups and solo performers and have been very successful doing so. I am most interested in aligning myself with a company such as Spinning Disc in order to work as a cooperative team member able to handle various artists simultaneously.

I have done extensive research in the industry and know that your company has an excellent work ethic, a client-centered approach to business, and solid integrity.

This industry is a challenging and exciting one, and requires hard work, persistence, and innovation, all qualities I possess. Again, the artists I currently represent are successful—testimony to my success in the business.

I look forward to meeting with you to discuss the possibilities for a mutually beneficial business arrangement. I will call June 3 to schedule an appropriate time for us to meet.

Sincerely,

Edna Thorson

Dear Sylvana Wong,

I am currently touring as a groom with Garson Stables and will be completing my circuit mid- September. At that time I would be interested to meet with you to discuss my skills and how I could benefit your stable.

I grew up on a farm and have worked with horses all my life. I consider myself lucky to have a career passion with such diversity. Having handled Thoroughbreds for nearly six years, I find I enjoy their high-spirited nature and the dynamic atmosphere the racetrack provides.

Your stable comes highly recommended and I am certain you would find me hard-working, positive and eager to learn.

I look forward to touring your facility and introducing myself in person. I will call the last week of August when I return to the city.

Sincerely,

David Davenport

KILEY THOMPSON

A good tennis pro is **knowledgeable, friendly, flexible** and **reliable.** I possess these qualities, as well as being an excellent tennis player.

I am very interested in providing lessons at your club during the summer. I will contact you on March 3 to discuss the opening you currently have for a tennis pro.

Kiley Thompson

(185) 555-9973

S ANDY ANDREWS

COMMITTED to helping sick and injured people

DEDICATED to my employer, my patients and myself

HARD-WORKING so patients receive the best care possible

If you want a nurse who loves helping people and finds the hustle and bustle of a busy hospital exhilarating, then I am the employee for you.

I am up-to-date on new technology and procedures and have training in many areas in acute care hospitals.

I would love the opportunity to demonstrate my skills and enthusiasm and look forward to speaking with you. I will call on June 11 to discuss a suitable time to speak with you.

Enthusiastically,

Sandy Andrews

(168) 555-9405

Dear Amie Giffen,

Thank you for taking time to talk with me on the phone Monday, April 4. I am certainly excited by the direction of your company and the upcoming events you have scheduled in your Public Relations department.

I have included a resume for your information. I would like to draw your attention to my continuing interest in public speaking and the variety of presentations I have given over the years and the variety of topics. I am a clear, concise, informative, and entertaining speaker and know my skills would easily adapt to your company and your clients.

I would enjoy meeting with you in person to discuss contributing to future projects with your company and will call the first of next week to schedule a convenient time for you.

Again, thank you for your time and your positive, encouraging, and professional outlook.

Sincerely,

Lynette Graham

Business Cards

Unique and effective business cards are a great way to familiarize employers with your name.

Develop a card which catches everyone's attention, not just employers but people who may know someone who is hiring. Give a card to everyone you know. If they meet someone who is looking for an employee, your business card can be passed on.

This is an inexpensive but effective way to let people know you are looking for work and to keep your name fresh in employers' minds.

 Look at your photo albums. Old pictures are fun to look at and remind us of good times.

Business Card Design

The same basic principles used in writing introductory letters apply when designing your business card.

- Be concise.

- Be interesting.

- Highlight your strongest skills and qualities.

- Emphasize your name and telephone number.

- Refer to the occupation you are interested in.

Have your business cards made professionally. If you have a computer, make them yourself. Always have some on hand wherever you go.

 Collect business cards from everyone you know. Not only will you have people's names, titles, and telephone numbers, you may get good ideas for your own business card.

Sample Business Cards

Business card ideas are presented on the following pages. When developing your card, use a format which is interesting and reflects your personality.

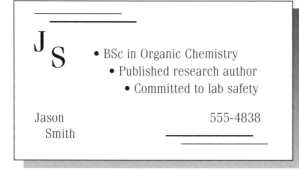

LOOKING??

For:
- A Team Player?
- A Dedicated Employee?
- Creativity and Innovation?

Arthur Van Hastings

——— 555-5844 ———

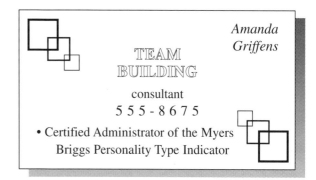

Amanda Griffens

TEAM BUILDING

consultant

5 5 5 - 8 6 7 5

- Certified Administrator of the Myers Briggs Personality Type Indicator

GILES REDMOND

DRAFTSMAN

- Experienced with AutoCad
- 8 years in construction design

555-6234

Topping Transport

Moving Your Product!

(416) 555-4829

Jason Topping Contractor

"Excellence in Communication"

- Specialization in Video Presentations

Jeanine Aron   555-8993

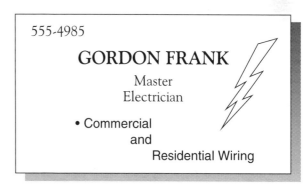

555-4985

GORDON FRANK

Master Electrician

- Commercial and
   Residential Wiring

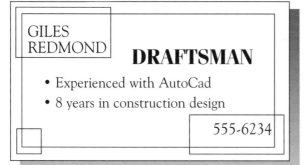

J S

- BSc in Organic Chemistry
  - Published research author
  - Committed to lab safety

Jason Smith   555-4838

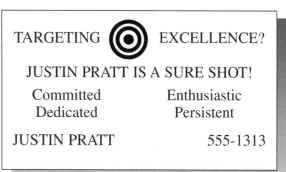

TARGETING  EXCELLENCE?

JUSTIN PRATT IS A SURE SHOT!

Committed   Enthusiastic
Dedicated   Persistent

JUSTIN PRATT   555-1313

rochures

Personalized job search brochures are another way to introduce yourself or remind employers of who you are. These eye-catching and unique tools will make you stand out in a crowd. Use them as a supplement to your resume, not as a replacement, and distribute them to the employers you want to make a strong impression with.

 "When writing ads, the shorter the headline the longer it stays in somebody's head."

—Tom Allen

Building Brochures

A brochure should not describe all your skills, but should instead emphasize your strongest qualities. Take a good look at yourself and determine what your most desirable skills are and briefly outline them in your brochure.

The thing to remember about brochures is that you do not have to be too wordy. A brief and to-the-point brochure is as effective as one with lengthy descriptions.

 Employers do not have a lot of time to read extra material so make sure what your brochure says is important, relevant, and has impact.

Sample Brochures

Create your own brochure, perhaps using ideas from the sample brochures on the following pages. Remember to personalize your brochure so that it reflects your skills and qualities.

"I'm only an average man but I work harder at it than the average man."

—Oliver Wendell Holmes

Which of Ken's Skills Can Benefit Your Team?

Networking/ Marketing Skills

- Developed large network base of private, not-for-profit and government agencies and businesses.

- Designed creative and innovative marketing tools for companies, programs and individual clients.

- Increased class enroll-ment by 40% through advertising and network-ing in person and over the telephone.

- Confident presenting myself and my ideas to individuals and organizations.

Communication Skills

- Experienced, dynamic public speaker: large groups, individuals, adults and teenagers.

- Excellent written com-munication skills: edited advertising, curricula, essays, speeches, resumes and cover letters.

- Knowledgeable in the use of IBM, compatibles and Macintosh comput-ers: WordPerfect, Microsoft Word 5.0, 5.1, Excel 4.0, and Pagemaker.

555-2121

brochure inside

What Can Ken Baines Offer XYZ Corporation of Dallas?

Ken Baines
Phone: 555-2121 (home)
556-3434 (work)

Creativity

- Proven ability to gener-ate creative ideas and solutions individually and in a team environ-ment.

Flexibility

- Excel in an environment where flexibility and diversification are essen-tial. Maintain an orga-nized approach to work load.

Enthusiasm

- Enjoy taking on new projects, meeting new people, and learning new things.

brochure cover

Brochure inside flap

Targeting Excellence?

Justin Pratt is a sure shot!

➤ **Committed**

➤ **Enthusiastic**

➤ **Dedicated**

➤ **Persistent**

**Justin Pratt
555-1313**

brochure inside

Justin Pratt

brochure cover

Bailey Cartwell

Developing workshops which assist parents in their child-rearing decisions is my love and passion. I am an excellent facilitator who encourages people to explore alternatives and make their own choices. I have strong communication skills, relate warmly to people, and enjoy one-on-one counseling. I have a great knowledge of community resources and am an excellent team player. These qualities along with my enthusiasm and professionalism make me a great counselor and workshop facilitator.

Bailey Cartwell

136 Expo Boulevard
Williston, North Dakota
35632

555-9613

brochure inside

**Bailey
Cartwell**

Parent Advisor

Workshop
Facilitator

555-9613

brochure cover

Area of Expertise:
Child Development

Credentials:
Bachelor of Science,
Specialization in
Psychology

Special Qualities:
Committed to Positive
Parenting Values

Truly concerned with
today's youth and the way
we influence them

Love of Children

Brochure inside flap

Food For Thought....

Ingredients
1 chef whole
a pinch of creativity,
a dash of innovation
5 years experience, well-seasoned
generous shake of positive attitude
leadership abilities, well-blended

Begin with the chef. Slowly add spices, stirring gently to allow the full flavor to
penetrate the mixture. Pour into the pot of a challenging and dynamic kitchen.
Let the mixture settle for a brief moment and bake. Watch it rise above all your
expectations. Serve while warm...enjoy.

Keith Montgomery

Sous Chef

brochure inside

Keith Montgomery

555-1357

brochure cover

31

Career-Specific Tools

You can use career-specific marketing tools to improve the impression you make on employers and increase the possibility of being hired. It is especially effective to provide concrete examples of the type of work you do.

Examples:

Occupation	Tool
Graphic Artist	Graphic Samples
Teacher	Sample Lesson Plan
Model	Picture Portfolio
Construction Blueprinter	Sample Blueprint
Sales/Marketing	Sales Strategy
Manager	Efficiency Ideas

 Have a double chocolate sundae on a hot day.

Thank-You Cards

Thank-you cards are an essential tool for your job search. Not only do they make people feel good, they also let people know you appreciate the time and effort they spent helping you. Someone who receives a thank-you is more likely to keep an eye open for you than someone who does not.

"The time is always right to do
what is right."

—Martin Luther King

Many people recognize the value of thank-you cards and send them. Make sure you are one of the people who sends a note, not one of the few who does not.

Put a birdfeeder outside your window and enjoy watching the birds which visit your home.

How?

Thank-yous are more personal than any other job search tool and express your appreciation in informal language. While it is not a good idea to handwrite any other job search tool, it is good when writing thank-yous.

Handwritten thank-yous give a personal touch. Typing up standard thank-yous makes people feel less appreciated. Take the time to write legibly.

To Whom?

Send thank-you cards to people who help with your job search. These include:

- employers you meet or speak with on the telephone.

- contacts who give you company and employer names.

- friends who let their friends know you are looking for work.

- organizations who help you in your search.

- anyone else who helps with your job hunt.

Examples:

Dear Blair Dains,

What a productive lunch we had Tuesday. It certainly has helped in my job search. I contacted two people you referred me to and have meetings with both of them next week. Thanks for your help.

Pat Schneider

Dear K.C. Thereoux,

Thank you for the time we spent discussing your company and its philosophies. Your eagerness and enthusiasm tell me your organization has great people working for them.

I will keep in touch.

Terri Randall

"I offered my services to the child-care center my son was attending. About a week later, the center asked me to come in for the day. Soon the work became full-time."

—Yvonne Armstrong, child-care worker

Dear Job Search Club Staff,

Your suggestions and guidance are truly appreciated. I feel more confident in my ability to obtain employment thanks to your help. I am open to further suggestions and contacts and look forward to hearing from you.

Renee Adams

Dear Jamie,

I know this may seem silly with us being good friends, but I wanted to tell you how much I appreciate your helping me find work.

Friends like you don't come around very often.

Darcy

Summing Things Up

"As I grow older, I pay less attention to what
men say. I just watch what they do."

—Andrew Carnegie

The resumes, brochures, business cards, and thank-you cards you
develop will be of great assistance in your job search. Now that you
have these useful and impressive tools, it's time to use them.

Chapter 3

The Job Hunt Starts at Home

It's important to prepare for and plan your job hunt so that things run smoothly. This will help you feel focused, and banish any "scattered" feeling you may have had during previous job hunts. The more you plan your job-hunting days, the more likely they are to end with you saying "That went well" rather than "I need a vacation!"

Write a letter to an old friend.

Were's My Pen?

The key to a successful job hunt is organization. It's hard to deliver resumes when you can't find them.

"I was working on the oil rigs and told friends I wanted to find a different job. A distributor from a snowboard company I knew of through previous jobs called and said they needed a representative. I went to company meetings and a few weeks later the international sales manager called and asked if I would be a representative."

—Scott Currie, snowboard representative

People who are employed begin their day by "checking in" at their designated work area. Accountants go to their desk, nurses go to the nursing station and drivers get in their vehicle; you need a work area for your job hunt as well.

Where?

Find an area in your house where you can work comfortably and privately, and designate it as your "work space." It's hard to speak with employers on the telephone when your children are using you as a human bridge.

 Do not locate your work space near the television. It's too easy to turn it on for a break and then forget to turn it off. Along with being distracting, the television is a great time-waster.

How?

Few people have the luxury of designating an entire room to their job search, so they "double up" on a room's duties. If your kitchen becomes your temporary office, it's important to set aside specific times for "non-kitchen duties."

Ask the rest of your household to respect your working time and space and refrain from interrupting you. This way everyone will be clear on when it's time to look for work and when it's time to cook dinner. (You can sneak an ice cream break without anyone knowing.)

 If you have children, arrange for babysitting when you are looking for work. Many states/provinces subsidize child-care expenses while people are job hunting. Check with your local employment agency.

Equipment?

Space is not the only job search requirement. You also need job hunting equipment.

Find an empty box to store your equipment. A box is portable, can be easily packed away, and, most importantly, keeps your materials together.

You will need:

- a *daily calendar* to schedule meetings and phonecalls and to record when you chat with people.

- an *address book* to record accurate names, titles, telephone numbers, and business addresses.

- *thank-you cards* to send to people who have helped you with your job search.

- several current *resumes,* to use as reference as well as to hand out to employers.

- a local *telephone book.*

- your *Contract Counter* to record significant information about conversations and meetings.

Use the Contact Counter provided at the end of this book to keep track of your contacts. If you stay organized you will be on top of your job search.

- *telephone* and *answering machine* (or at least a phone number where people can leave messages).

- *pens.*

- *paper.*

Arrange to have access to a typewriter or computer on a regular basis, and use it to update resumes, information letters, etc.

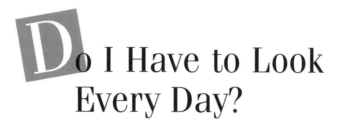o I Have to Look Every Day?

Although the rule of thumb is *"treat your job search like a job,"* each person has their own tolerance level for seeking employment. If you can manage looking for work on a full time basis, that's wonderful, go for it. But if you periodically need a break, that's okay, too.

"After receiving my child care diploma, I walked into a child care center where I was interested in working. I said I would volunteer for the day and they could see how I worked. During that same day, they said I could do relief work. When a job came up I went through the formal application process and was hired full time."

—Y. Earley, Child Care Worker

Schedule at least three days per week to be job-seeking days.

- Monday is a day you must dedicate to your job hunt. It will get your week started on the right track and you can catch employers before they schedule their entire week.

- Tuesday, Wednesday and Thursday are optional days, although it's best, of course, to look for work as much as you can.

- Friday mornings are all right, but the afternoons are not the most productive times. Employers are winding down their week and are hard to reach.

If you speak with someone on a Friday afternoon, they are often tired and less willing to help you than if you had called on a different day.

Each person has their own peak performance days and times. Think about when yours are and schedule your job search for these times. Be at your peak when job searching, not when napping.

 Take a break on the days you have scheduled off. Use this time to regenerate and focus on other things so that you will feel rejuvenated when it is time to get back into your job hunt.

Treat your job search like a real job, because *it is*.

- Schedule appointments.

- Take coffee and lunch breaks.

- Begin "work" at 9:00 a.m. and finish at 4 or 5 p.m.

- Be productive. Although you may have to sit and think at times, don't let your thinking time outweigh your working time.

Develop a routine similar to one you would have if you were employed.

Monday	Look for work
Monday night	Go to the gym
Tuesday	Day off; run errands
Wednesday	Look for work
Thursday	Look for work
Thursday night	Slow pitch game
Friday	Afternoon; read a book

Not only does this make the transition easier once you begin working, it also gives you something to do each day.

Chapter 4

What Hidden Job Market!?

Everywhere you look, every course you take, and every book or newspaper you pick up tells you about the hidden job market and how you must access it to land the job of your dreams. In the last eight to ten years, the hidden job market has been the focus of much discussion. Statistics show that allegedly 75 percent of jobs are not listed, but must be accessed through the hidden job market.

What Do They Mean?

The hidden job market simply refers to jobs not listed or advertised in a conventional manner. These include:

- newspaper ads.

- company job boards/computer banks.

- career papers.

- phone-in employment lines.

"What I'm looking for is a blessing
not in disguise."

—Kitty O'Neill Collins

Why Do Companies Use It?

A company often chooses not to advertise a position simply to avoid the time-consuming work and responsibility that accompanies the hiring process. A company looking for employees must cope with dozens, if not hundreds, of phone calls and people dropping by the office. This cuts into the productive time of current employees who must answer these calls and be interrupted by walk-ins. Additionally, interviews must be scheduled and employee time allotted for screening and interviewing potential candidates.

With limited time and money to dedicate to hiring new employees, companies often employ innovative methods to screen the overwhelming flood of applicants they receive for any given position.

 To gain an idea of the competition in your field, make a point of asking how many applications have been received when you submit your resume.

Screening Method 1

A personnel manager faced with a stack of 400 resumes for a national sales position, and lacking the time and staff to read every resume, devised a method of screening applications. The following were screened out of the competition:

- those without a cover letter.
- those who folded their resume into a small letter-sized envelope. (It was too difficult to take them out, unfold them and then have them lie flat in the pile.)
- those without dynamic 'sales oriented' words in their cover letter.

By the time these initial screening techniques were complete, only 150 resumes remained to be screened for specific qualifications!

"Continuous effort - not strength or intelligence - is the key to unlocking our potential."

—Liane Cordes

Screening Method 2

A local manufacturing company had openings for 12 staff to begin production in a new outlet. These positions were non-specialized, but the salary and hours were very good. The hiring staff received 1000 applications. How did they face the impossible task of selection? Someone stood at the top of a flight of stairs with a pile of resumes and applications and threw them down! Those that landed on the first few stairs were those that were called in!

This is by no means a common scenario. More often than not someone will at least personally review your resume.

Although this seems like a bizarre and unfair way to select suitable candidates, don't let it depress or frustrate you. It simply illustrates how important it is for you to do everything possible to make your job search unique and successful.

Do everything you can to make an employer's task of looking at your resume quick and easy. Make your resume and cover letter easy to read, staple pages together (paper clips fly off and pages separate), and hand deliver it in an 8 1/2 x 11, unsealed envelope or no envelope at all (no effort is then needed to rip it open). Anything you do to make your application accessible will benefit you!

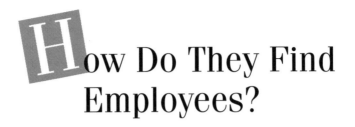How Do They Find Employees?

So how does a company find appropriate staff?

Networking

Smaller companies often pass the word around their organization and the organizations they do business with to see if anyone knows of a suitable candidate. This way they are somewhat familiar with the candidate before an interview. If a trusted employee recommended this candidate, there is already a built-in reference.

 "It's a simple formula; do your best and somebody might like it."

—Dorothy Baker

In-store Signs

This method is often used in retail stores. Signs are placed in windows and at front desks to attract the attention of people who frequent the establishment. With an in-store sign, word gets around, the store avoids the high cost of advertising, and people who frequent the business are aware there is a position available.

 Rent a movie and make popcorn. Better yet, invite some people over and make an evening of it.

Head Hunters/Professional Recruiters

This method is often used by larger companies looking for employees to work in their organization. Because the company is often looking for specialized staff, they will hire the services of a professional recruiter familiar with the position and the company's needs. The recruiter's responsibility is to approach people they feel would meet the needs of the company.

 Head hunters make it their business to be familiar with "up and comers" in the business, and make great efforts to network and familiarize themselves with individuals working within that industry.

Employment/Staffing Agencies

By using an employment agency a company can still advertise their staffing needs, but the phone number and address of the agency are listed. The employment agency fields all resumes, walk-ins, and phonecalls for information, which saves the hiring company considerable time and expense.

 "The man who removes a mountain begins by carrying away small stones."

—Chinese Proverb

How Do I Access This Hidden Market?

NETWORK!

Get to know as many people as you can and tell as many people as will listen that you are looking for work. Above all, be prepared.

- Have business cards made and pass them out.

- Design an informative brochure and pass out copies.

- Keep your resume current at all times.

- Go to every interview you schedule.

- Keep in touch with people you have met.

 Look in your local telephone directory for a relevant association to help get your networking started.

Example

Recently, Chris interviewed for a position she was very excited about. When she didn't get the job she was disappointed but moved on in her job search. Not long after, she was hired elsewhere. After a week in her new job another employer called and left a message at her home. Her name had been given to him by the same employer who had decided not to hire her but was nevertheless impressed enough to recommend her to a friend. What did she do? In the spirit of never slamming any doors and keeping all options open, she went to the interview and decided to accept the new position for a bigger salary!

This is how the hidden job market works. Employers talk to each other and employees recommend friends and associates for job openings.

 "Success is getting what you want. Happiness is wanting what you get."

—Carl Trumbell Hayden

You need to learn to talk to people about what you are looking for and where you are looking. Sooner or later, someone will remember a meeting they had with you and will pass your name to the right person. Don't let opportunities pass you by!

Chapter 5

Cultivating Contacts

Often one of the most difficult and foreign concepts when you are about to undertake a serious job search is the idea of networking: personally meeting people who can help you with your job search. If you have been employed for some time, you may not have ever had to network or work hard at finding employment. If you have been in school for a number of years, you may also be unfamiliar with the effort and skills needed to secure employment. Or, if you have not had to look for work recently, you may still be unfamiliar with the new methods essential to gaining meaningful employment. Whatever your situation, it will take some adjustment before you get your job search routine underway.

"Be patient with everyone, but above all with yourself."

—St. Francis De Sales

Becoming A Master Networker

You have heard over and over that you must learn to network in order to have a successful job search. But where do you start?

"Opportunities are usually disguised as hard work, so most people don't recognize them."

—Barbara Rowe

Stretching My Comfort Zone

You must realize that in order to succeed and become a "master networker" you will have to expand, or leave, your personal comfort zone. Everyone has certain areas in their lives where they feel comfortable and confident with themselves, their abilities, and the people around them. This is their comfort zone.

To get outside it means picking up the phone and calling someone you feel may not have the time or the desire to talk to you. It may mean telling people you normally wouldn't tell such things to that you are unemployed and looking for a specific type of work.

 Leaving your comfort zone to network with new people is probably the most important and most difficult challenge you will face during your job search. But it is also the most rewarding.

"You must do the thing you think you cannot do."

—Eleanor Roosevelt

Circles of Influence

Through daily living and regular interaction with people, you have a group of individuals you know on a first name basis, know through friends, or know on a casual basis: these are your circles of influence. Generally, you have three different circles of influence:

 Think of this concept as a bull's-eye. Your hot circle of influence is in the center and the warm and cold circles are the outer circles.

Hot Circle

The hot circle contains people you speak to and interact with on a regular basis.

This group includes family, close friends, and other individuals you feel comfortable dealing with in person. These people are easy to approach and you should have no trouble "networking" with them.

 Find a massage school where students give massages. It's always cheaper and sometimes free. Indulge!

Warm Circle

As you move outward and away from the people you regularly interact with, you move toward and into a larger circle. Here you find people you may have worked with at one time, acquaintances, and friends of friends.

You may not be completely at ease speaking to these people one-on-one, but at least you've seen them around. Still, you can comfortably approach many of the people in your warm circle. A casual introduction from a friend or a phone call from a mutual friend to let them know who you are will make it easier. This circle of influence is definitely larger than your hot circle, and its one you will need to access if your job search is to be successful.

Make a list of *all* the people you can think of. You will be amazed at the size of your network already.

Cold Circle

Your cold circle is the largest circle available for your search. Simply put, it's all the people you do not know personally.

Often these are people you have heard of or admire but would never consider speaking to because you feel intimidated or believe they would not have the time for you. Your cold circle could include anyone from a local politician to the president of the human resources department at a corporation you are interested in working for.

Take yourself out to watch some local amateur sports. You'll support a good cause, have a good time, and probably meet new people.

Statistics show the average person knows at least 2000 people on a first name basis. THIS is the power of your network. While you are looking for employment you must constantly expand and use your network, your circles of influence.

ho Do I Call?

Start with your hot circle.

Again, these are people you are comfortable with, the people who care about you: close friends, family, relatives, past employers, etc. Take advantage of their genuine willingness to help you:

- tell them what type of work you are looking for.

- ask who they know who could be of help to your search.

- ask that they introduce you to their friends, their hot circle of influence.

- talk to them when you feel low and need support.

- ask for their feedback on resumes, cover letters and other job search tools you have created.

 "Have courage to act instead of react."

—Darlene Larsen Jenko

At the outset of your job search you must make a point to speak in person with everyone in your hot circle. Be sure to keep in close contact with these people as you continue your search. Your network is beginning to expand!

 "I was to have lunch with the "friend of a friend" I had recently met. He called me to cancel our appointment because his video production manager had quit and he needed to find someone to fill the job. I said, "Hire me" and he did!"

—PJ Mattia, Production Manager

Stretch to your warm circle.

When you have approached all the people in your hot circle and have made note of all the people they think may help you, move on to your warm circle of influence. These are acquaintances, people you know on a casual first name basis. This circle is much larger than your hot circle.

 When you have a job, make a point of writing down the names, phone numbers, and positions of people you know in the workplace. You never know when this list will come in handy.

First you need to make appointments and schedule informal meetings with the people your hot circle introduced you to.

Next, you need to alert others in your warm circle that you are looking for work:

- Call people you used to work with, find out where they work now, and ask if their company is looking for help. Don't limit your discussions to only those people you worked with. Think of salespeople who came to your office, contract workers who offered temporary services, and other people you associated with in the industry. Be sure to leave them one of your creative brochures.

- Call former employers to let them know you are in the market. Ask them to put you in touch with people they know, and leave them a copy of your resume.

- Tell the people you do volunteer work with that you are looking for work. Ask them to tell their friends. If you aren't currently a volunteer at any organization, this is a good time to start.

- Tell your bankteller, doctor, grocery clerk, hairdresser, etc., that you are looking for work. You may be surprised who they will be able to introduce you to. These are the perfect people to leave business cards with.

Always have a business card or brochure with you. You never know who you might meet!

Expand to your cold circle.

This is where it gets exciting. By now you should have lots of practice and the appointments are lining up. It's time to move into your cold circle of influence, the largest circle available to build into your personal network. Ideally, you've become more and more comfortable with the idea of meeting and networking with new people.

At this point you should:

• Continue to talk to people in your warm circle. This is a big circle of people and one that will certainly benefit you in the long term.

• Use your Contact Counter (described in Chapter 6) to keep track of all the people you are talking to and giving your resume, brochure, or business card to.

• Make a point of touching base with people periodically, even though they may not have been able to help you when you first approached them. They may come up with ideas, information, or suggestions for you as time goes on.

• Be sure you are keeping appointments and continually scheduling new ones.

 "With each new day I put away the past and discover the new beginnings I have been given."
—Angela L. Wozniak

If you use your warm circle of influence effectively, you may not even have to move on to your cold circle. Now that you are becoming a "master networker," though, you should be excited by the opportunities and resources available to you.

How?

1. Education

    Take a course with your local school board. These classes are affordable and are a great way to meet new people.

"I stated in my cover letter that I was an alumnus at the college where I was seeking employment. When I delivered my resume, I spoke with the Vice President, who remembered me from when I was a student. I was hired in a temporary position which eventually became full-time. It was my credentials which eventually got me the job, but being an alumnus got me in the door."

—Marilyn Grabinsky, project coordinator

2. Volunteer

    Choose something you are interested in or, even better, something related to your chosen field. There are countless examples of volunteer positions turning into paid ones. Even if that doesn't happen, you will still meet interesting people who may surprise you with their genuine interest in helping you with your career search.

3. Through Your Children

    Become involved in your children's activities. Coach their teams, help out at various functions, or just go and watch. There are always other parents there and you never know who you will meet and the suggestions and assistance they can offer.

Round up your kids and go for a picnic.

4. Community Involvement

   Pursue your interests in the community theatre, poetry readings, public speaking groups, or whatever else you enjoy. Often these groups are available at a minimal cost and are a great way to meet people on a casual basis.

 Not only do you get out and socialize, boosting your morale when you need it, you are turning your cool circle of influence into your warm circle!

5. Sports

   No matter where you live or what the climate, there are always sporting activities of some sort available for every interest. Join a walking club, community volleyball, or summer slow pitch league. Get adventurous and learn to scuba dive or hang glide! The physical activity will do you a world of good and you will meet people with similar interests, people who may turn out to be invaluable contacts.

QRW

"I had been sending out unsolicited resumes and, while working out, I happened to meet a woman who worked at one of the schools I applied to. She let me know something was coming up, gave me some inside information about the hiring procedure and the interview, and put in a good word with her supervisor for me. It turned out I didn't get the position. However, the woman who was hired took another position and, as I was their second choice, they called me after all!"

—E.D. Bailey

"If it weren't for the fact that the TV set and the refrigerator are so far apart, some of us wouldn't get any exercise at all."

—Joey Adams

6. Church

   More and more churches are moving toward social, non-denominational functions, focusing on the feeling of community. There are all sorts of activities offered through local churches. This makes for a non-threatening, supportive atmosphere to become involved with your community, meet some new people, and have some fun.

You must join a group that interests you. If you join only because you know you have to and this seems as good a group as any, you certainly won't enjoy yourself and that will be clear to the rest of the group. This is not the impression you want to create among a group of people who may potentially help you gain employment. Also, it will be difficult for you to continue going and painful for you to make the effort to meet people. Get involved in something you enjoy!

7. Associations

   Look in your local community directory and you will find an endless list of associations. There are associations for virtually every profession and interest group out there. Phone around to find out what the cost and guidelines are for joining the association relevant to your situation.

There are professional associations for:

- Human Resource Professionals

- Nurses

- Writers

- Lawyers

- Carpenters

- Painters

The list is endless, you could even start your own if you wish!

 "Having it all doesn't necessarily mean having it all at once."

—Stephanie Luetkehans

There are associations for specialty interest groups:

- Women in the media

- Community sports

- Mentally handicapped individuals

- Seniors' friendship centers

The list goes on... Get involved!

Often there are groups that get together specifically to network. If you check with your local chamber of commerce or labor market library, they may be able to offer some suggestions and point you in the right direction. These groups often have breakfast meetings, after-business mixers, or casual social gatherings with guest speakers or other entertainment. Shop around. You will be sure to find something that suits you and your needs.

Don't run out and join every association and group you can find and then become frustrated when you don't instantly meet those people who can land you your dream job. This is a process that takes time. Be persistent, enjoy yourself along the way, and it will pay off.

8. Trade Shows or Industry Exhibitions

Trade shows, industry fairs, and exhibitions are a great way to meet people involved in the kind of work you are looking for. Since the job market is becoming so focused on education and employee training, many industries are coordinating trade fairs to exhibit the new technology, equipment, training, or direction for their particular field. Sometimes these are all-day events complete with displays, speakers, networking luncheons, and seminars. At other times they may be weekend events.

 "Where I is is where I is–but where I'm going is up to me."

—Charles J. Givens, Superself

Regardless of the length of time, these exhibitions are often open to the public and are an excellent way to meet people involved with the business that interests you. Take advantage of these events whenever you can. It is always to your benefit to be seen by people in your field, to remind them you are still around and that you are keeping current with the job and are interested enough to take the time to participate in industry-sponsored events. In addition, you may discover an aspect of the business you weren't aware of that could expand your job possibilities!

 Now that you belong to a relevant association, they should be able to keep you current on what events are coming to town.

Be absolutely certain to take along business cards and brochures to these events. Make it a personal goal to meet at least five people each day, get their business card and, whenever possible, make an appointment to meet with them after the event. Smile, take a deep breath, and jump in!

 Jot down on the back of the business card who this person is, where you met them, what you discussed, and any comments they offered. This will be useful in the future.

 Pick a project you've been meaning to get to for a while and complete it. It will give you that great feeling of accomplishment.

9. Internships

An internship involves offering your services to a company for a period of a few days, free of cost to the employer. Obviously this is not possible in every industry, but if it's an option in your field, go for it! Think of it as a trial period.

 You are the resident expert in your line of work. Only you know if it is feasible to offer yourself as an intern.

You could try and set up an internship if:

- you are interested in working for a company and believe that if they could see how you worked they would hire you.

- this is a new division of an industry you have been in for a while and you aren't yet sure if you would like to pursue it full-time.

- this is a new company and you aren't sure if you want to work for them.
- you don't have a lot of contacts in the industry and need to establish some.

You may approach an employer, explain your situation, and offer your services on a trial run. Some employers are thrilled, some are not. Often those that are not are short-staffed and feel it would take productive time away from their other employees to train you. This is the time to sell them on your ability to take initiative on your own and to learn very quickly!

 It may help your case when meeting a potential sponsor employer if you outline what you hope to gain from an internship and what benefit there would be for the employer.

Summing It Up

There are many different ways to meet people who have the potential to help you with your search.

Be creative. Try to do things in an innovative, yet still professional way, so people remember and find you interesting.

Be positive. Your attitude is contagious. If people find you a pleasure to be around they will be more willing to help you.

Be persistent. Don't expect miracles overnight. This will take time and you will have setbacks. Keep at it and you will succeed.

Now . . . go for it!

"The will to win is not nearly as important as the will to prepare to win."

—Bobby Knight

How Do I Approach People?

For some, meeting people in a business context may be a new experience. For others it may be familiar. Either way, before you begin your approach you should have an idea of what you are planning to say.

How you approach someone from your hot circle and what you say to them will be different from how you approach and speak to someone in your cold circle, simply because of how you feel about doing it. Obviously you are more comfortable and confident with people you know!

Go to the playground with your kids—borrow some if you don't have any—and play on the swings with them!

Approaching Your Hot Circle

This is the easy one. You know the people in your hot circle well and probably have a good idea of how you would like them to help you. Perhaps you have a friend with a computer who could help you with business cards. Maybe your father golfs with someone who works in the type of position you would like to work in. Perhaps your brother-in-law is starting a business and needs some help that you think you are qualified to offer. The possibilities are there. You simply have to do a little talking.

Take the time to decide exactly what it is you are looking for before you talk to people. It is impossible for them to help if all you can tell them about what you are looking for is "I'd like to work with kids."

Just Do It

Begin talking to people in your hot circle as soon as you possibly can. They can offer you much-needed support as well as suggestions at the outset of your career search. Make sure, however, you talk to them in a comfortable situation. Meet with them when they have time to sit down and talk with you, not when they are running out the door or concentrating on something else. The meeting can be an informal one, such as a chat across the kitchen table, but it must be a focused one nonetheless. This is your job search and it is important.

Try and give people a little advance notice of what you would like from them. This will give them time to consider what names and suggestions they can offer you.

You may be surprised by the willingness and ability of your hot circle of influence to help you. All you need to do is ask.

The Script

You may have more productive meetings if you write down what you want to say to people before you call or approach them. This should be just an outline, not something you read word-for-word over the phone.

Remember, you know the people in your hot circle well and have a good idea of how they can help you. What you say to each of them will vary from person to person.

"If you don't know where you are going, you will probably end up somewhere else."

—Laurence J. Peter

SCRIPT ONE

Hi Mary. I'm not sure if you heard or not but I've been laid off from XYZ corporation so I'm out hunting for work again. I remember you used an employment service last year when you were looking for work so I thought I'd give you a call and get their name and any other suggestions you might have.

"Give people as much specific information as possible. There is nothing worse than hearing, after it's too late, "Oh, I could have introduced you to that person, but I didn't think you would be interested.""

SCRIPT TWO

Chris, how are things? The reason I'm calling is to ask you to wrack your brain for names of people you know in the computer repair business that I could talk to about doing an internship. I'm interested in making a career change and would appreciate any ideas you have.

SCRIPT THREE

Hello Pat, what's on your schedule for next week? I'd like to get together and chat about all the people you know from that public speaking group you belong to. I'm looking for work in public relations so I thought a public speaking group would be a great place to start networking. Gee, maybe I'll even join!

63

"If you want your place in the sun you've got to put up with a few blisters."

—Abigail Van Buren

Approaching Your Warm Circle

Remember, these are still people you know: acquaintances, friends of friends, and now, all the people you just finished meeting through introductions from your hot circle!

You want to contact all the people you possibly can. Don't edit someone off your list just because you don't think they will be able to offer any help. You never know who they know!

QRW

"Three years ago I was involved in negotiations for a new phone system for our company. I was responsible for liaising with the phone installation and service company that ultimately won the bid. Four months ago the manager of that company called me and asked if I was bound to a contract where I worked. I said no. We had lunch and discussed his needs and how I could fit into their organization. I gave notice that week at my old job."

—Marnie Braund

Remember to keep in touch with everyone you meet, even if they can't offer any help immediately. You never know how the situation might change.

"Be prepared when you call to speak on the phone to a potential contact. People are busy. You do not want to waste their time.

Take A Breath and Get Started

Sometimes the hardest part of getting in touch with people is picking up the phone and making the first call of the day. Do whatever you can to motivate yourself and sound positive before you make the first call:

• Splash your face with cold water.

• Brush your teeth.

• Run around the block.

• Read the comic strip.

• Review your resume.

• Tell yourself in the mirror how great you are.

• Make a quick call to an upbeat friend.

Try as often as possible to meet people in person. It is much harder to say "no," or "I'm sorry I can't help you" to someone sitting across from you than it is over the phone.

Are you ready? Now pick up the phone.

"We first make our habits, and then our habits make us."

—John Dryden

The Script

Here are some examples of how to approach people you don't know well.

SCRIPT ONE

Hello James, my name is Chris Sebert. I'm not sure if you remember me, but we met last month at the Small Fries little league game. I happened to be sitting next to you and we were chatting about youth counseling.

 Hopefully, he remembers you. If not, don't be discouraged. Try to jog his memory a bit more and if he still doesn't remember you, ask to meet with him anyway. You might as well, since you've got him on the phone and he'll remember you when he sees you.

Right! My kid hit the home run! Anyway, James, I know you're busy. The reason I'm calling is I'm looking for work as a youth counselor and wondered if you had 15 minutes some time this week when we could get together and chat. I thought you might know of someone who was hiring or have some ideas or suggestions about who else I could contact. Sure, Tuesday would be great. See you then.

SCRIPT TWO

Hello Margaret, my name is Martin Woo. A mutual friend of ours, Deanne Lane, suggested I give you a call. I recently graduated from law school and am looking for work. I wonder if we might get together some time this week for 15 minutes to discuss the possibility of working for your firm, or if you know of any other firms that are looking. I would appreciate any suggestions or help you can give me. Thank you very much.

Dress appropriately when making your calls. You'll sound more professional dressed in a suit than when you are in a bathrobe and slippers.

SCRIPT THREE

Hello Cory, my name is Robin Davies. We met last week at the boat and trailer show. I stopped in at your company booth and you gave me a business card and suggested I call. I'm hoping you have the time this week to get together and discuss some of the avenues you think I could take in the RV Business. Your company seemed like an industry pioneer and you certainly had a lot of ideas. Wednesday for lunch would be great. Thanks, Cory.

Don't be discouraged if not everyone you call is interested in meeting with you. People are busy and sometimes they simply don't have the time to spare. If you can't set up a meeting in person, ask the person if there is a better time to call them back. Perhaps they can suggest someone else you should call.

 Never hang up the phone without either an appointment scheduled or having asked if they know of anyone else you might contact.

If you feel you are not getting any positive responses from the people you call, try out your script on some friends, and get constructive feedback. Make positive adjustments. The near misses you've had were simply a sign that you needed to readjust your course, not an indication that you've wasted your time.

If your friends think you sound positive and professional, keep at it. Eventually you will speak to someone who will give you a break!

 Make a videotape of short comedic routines, TV bloopers, or funny sitcoms. Whenever you feel low, plug in the tape and have a laugh!

Approaching Your Cold Circle

Now that you have practice talking with people on the phone and setting up appointments, you are more than ready to move on to your cold circle of influence.

 Already you have probably moved people from your cold circle to your warm circle just by asking acquaintances to introduce you to people they know!

Congratulations on learning how to network!

 "I was new in town and didn't know anyone, so I picked up the telephone directory and called companies listed there. I introduced myself and my experience, and the second number I called was a company where someone had just gone on extended sick leave. The manager asked me to drop by with my resume and I started work the next day."

—Dakota Field, senior's recreation coordinator

Be Prepared

Be prepared to answer questions about yourself, your skills, and your experience, especially when you are talking to people you have never met. These people are going to want to know a bit about you before they decide if it is worth their time to meet with you. They will absolutely want to know about you before they risk their reputation and refer you to their industry contacts.

Do not be offended by their need to know who you are. If they are going to allow you to use their name when you introduce yourself to their colleagues, they must be sure you are someone they are comfortable being associated with.

You **must** be prepared to tell people briefly, but effectively, why you are a valuable employee who can be recommended to anyone.

Keep in mind that you need to:

- motivate and energize yourself before picking up the phone.

- dress professionally and speak positively.

- have a resume in front of you for reference.

- sell yourself, convincing your contacts that it is in their best interest to see you.

- respect that people are busy and be brief and to the point.

- try not to hang up the phone without either obtaining an appointment or another name to call.

- drop off a resume with a cover letter reminding them of your telephone conversation.

- send a quick thank-you note.

 "Life is like an ice cream cone. You have to lick it one day at a time."

—Charlie Brown

Get A Name

There are two different scenarios you may encounter when you begin circulating in your cold circle and calling companies and potential employers.

Perhaps you don't have a contact name, but know you are interested in working for a particular company. Or maybe you do have a contact name with someone within the organization but have not yet been introduced. You may have simply called the company and asked who you should speak with.

How you approach a company will vary depending on whether or not you know who to contact.

"I had made as many contacts as I could through my personal network, so I started to call companies out of the phonebook. On the third call I chatted with the owner of a company who wasn't looking for anyone, but he was so impressed with my introduction on the phone he suggested I deliver my resume and come in for an interview. I went that afternoon and he offered me a job he had created for me on the spot!

—Denise Marcotte, photographer

If you do not have anyone specific to speak with at your target company, getting a name is your first priority.

How?

1. Call the personnel office to inquire about positions available.

   • This is the least effective method. The personnel office is not always completely aware of what is happening in each department until staff must be hired. You need to meet people and sell yourself before positions are advertised.

2. Call the department you wish to work in and ask to speak to the manager.

   • Even if you've reached a person involved in the work that interests you, they still may not be the most appropriate or fruitful contact.

3. Call the department, explain to the receptionist that you are looking for work, and ask who they think you should speak with.

- This is often a good starting point. The receptionist usually refers you to someone willing to take the time to answer your questions.

 In today's job market, the majority of new positions are found in small businesses. When you call a small business you may need to speak to only one person. That person might well be the owner, manager, and personnel officer!

Regardless of who you speak to initially when you call a large organization, you will probably be passed along to several different people before you meet the person who can really help you. Do not be discouraged by this. You want to speak to the person most closely associated with the job you would like to have, so be patient and impress as many people along the way as you can!

 Keep a list of names of all the people in the organization you speak to. When you make your second call to that company it is nice to be able to say, "Ms. Z, the manager in the X department, suggested that I call you."

Eventually you'll have the name of someone specific to speak with. Whether or not this person is the last one you need to speak with remains to be seen, but it is a starting point.

The Script

You may find that you are a little nervous and uncomfortable on your first few phone calls. After you have a better idea of what people tend to ask and what you want and need to say, you will probably revise your approach and it will become smooth and polished. Do not read from a prepared speech when you are speaking on the phone. Inevitably, they won't say what you were expecting and you will become frustrated and flustered because they do not fit into your carefully prepared script.

"Do prepare an opening sentence or two. The first few seconds is when a potential employer decides if they even want to continue with you on the phone. Have a general idea of what you would like to say during the rest of the conversation, but do not be so concerned about reading your script that you can't answer the questions you are asked.

See if any of the following examples can serve as inspiration for your own approach.

SCRIPT ONE

Hello Mr. Pritchard, my name is Hamish Stevens. I'm calling because I am changing directions in my career and looking at some of the opportunities that are available. I have worked as a newspaper editor for five years and am interested in expanding into editing for a book publisher. I thought I would give you a call and discuss the possibilities of employment with your company.

At this point Mr. Pritchard will decide if he wants to talk to you further, pass you along to someone else, or tell you he and his company are not interested.

SCRIPT TWO

Hello Ms. Mosher. My name is Hamish Stevens. Mr. Pritchard gave me your name and suggested I call you. I am an editor and I'm looking for work in the book publishing industry. I have five years experience as a newspaper editor so I am used to a fast-paced environment with strict deadlines. I am interested in learning more about your company and the possibilities of working with you. I wondered if you might have 15 minutes this week when we could meet?

It is an excellent idea to set a time limit to your proposed meeting. When employers realize you are not asking for an hour of their precious time, they may be more receptive.

Now it is Ms. Mosher's turn to decide what direction your relationship will go. For interest's sake, let's say she tells you there are no openings currently and she is simply too busy to meet with you.

That's fine. I understand the hectic nature of the business. (Stay positive!) May I pop by in the next day or two and drop off a resume for you in case something opens up in the future? That would be great. Is there a time that would be best? Thanks very much for your time.

"Who dares nothing, need hope for nothing."

—Johann von Schiller

OK, no problem. I certainly understand how busy editors can be. I wonder if you have any ideas or suggestions of other people I might call? Excellent, thank you. (Scribble, scribble...the sound of you frantically writing down the names she gave you.) Thanks very much Ms. Mosher, I appreciate your help. I wonder if I might stop in and give you a resume just in case something comes up? All right, I will do that. Thank you again.

 Always have a pen and paper by the phone to jot down names, phone numbers, and any other relevant information. It is also handy to help you remember the name of the person you are speaking with!

Remember these suggestions are only basic outlines for your initial contact with people. You will definitely have to do this in a way that's comfortable for you. Make sure you do it! Above all be prepared. Nine times out of ten an employer will ask you what you are good at or why they should see you. Sell yourself!

Summing It Up

Some of your conversations will leave you feeling encouraged. Unfortunately, some of them will leave you feeling depressed and negative. Don't let these ones get to you. Indulge in a Blues Buster and get back at it. With persistence and practice you will become a "master networker." You will land that job!

Chapter 6

Is There Help Out There?

Ultimately, success in your job search is up to you, but there are places you can go for help and agencies designed to make your search a little less painful. By all means enlist the help of these services. You may gain valuable information and make some excellent contacts. Remember, however, that you are ultimately responsible for your success. Looking for work is challenging and sometimes frustrating, but you can't rely on someone else to do it for you. The only way you will be pleased with the results is if you are in control.

"To be upset over what you don't have is to waste what you do have."

—Ken S. Keyes, Jr.

There are various services available to assist people in their job search. Most services are open to everyone, but some government-funded programs have restrictions on who may be admitted.

Research which services are available in your area and assess them according to your needs. Take into account your:

- job search timeline.

- financial situation.

- need for assistance and guidance.

- access to contacts/network.

- personal level of motivation.

- state of mind (could you use the support group).

You will also need to consider their:

- fee for service.

- eligibility requirements.

- time commitment requirements.

- type of program and if it will benefit you.

- professional staff.

 Often the best way to choose a service is to be referred by someone who has used it. Ask to speak to current students or graduates of a program before making your decision.

If you decide to use a service, be sure to shop around for the one that best fits your needs.

ho Do I Contact?

There are many services available to help you with your job search. These include:

1. Government Employment Centers

   - They are often walk-in centers.

   - The staff is able to make referrals.

   - Job openings are posted for various employers.

   - Their services are free.

   - May offer basic resume writing and interview skill workshops.

   - Make referrals to more in-depth programs.

RATINGS:

✓ Often have specialized services for students.

✓ Good places to start.

✓ Often able to provide referrals to programs which better suit your needs.

– Jobs which are high-paying, permanent, or specialized are often filled within a few days. You must check listings frequently.

"When everything seems to be going against you, remember that the airplane takes off against the wind, not with it."

—Henry Ford

2. Job Clubs

• Privately run or government-funded organizations.

• Usually run for three weeks.

• Designed for intensive job searches.

• Sometimes offer interview skill training.

• May require a resume prior to enrollment or create one with you.

• Days are spent calling employers and scheduling appointments.

• Staff available to assist you.

• Full days, Monday to Friday.

• You can leave the program early if you gain employment.

RATINGS

✓ Excellent for motivation and job search discipline.

– Very quick programs. Sometimes you aren't able to learn the process thoroughly enough to be able to continue on your own.

3. Government-Funded Programs

- Usually, but not always, last longer than job clubs.

- May include classroom time, i.e. interview skills, communication skills, salary negotiation, resume writing, and computer skills.

- Some programs are specialized to industry, i.e. only accept people interested in becoming a chef or those who want to work in the hospitality industry.

- Often you must be receiving some kind of financial assistance from the government to be eligible.

- You must go through a screening process before being accepted.

- Full days, Monday to Friday.

- Professional staff available to assist you.

- Can leave the program early if you gain employment.

RATINGS:

✓ Excellent skill training.

✓ Excellent support group.

✓ You must do the work on your own.

− You must work at the pace of the group, which can be frustrating.

"A bad habit never disappears miraculously: it's an undo-it-your-self project."

—Abigail Van Buren

4. Temporary Placement Agencies

- Many to choose from in larger cities.

- Agencies often specialize in particular occupations.

- You may register with as many as you like.

- You may be required to take a skill test of some sort.

- There is usually no fee to join—the employer pays your salary to the agency and they take a percentage.

- Normally do not offer services or classes such as resume writing.

RATINGS:

✓ You are exposed to the agency's contacts.

✓ Temporary work offers a good opportunity to get your foot in the door of a company and network.

– Some people rely on agencies to be their only form of job search.

– An agency may have too many clients and you get lost in the shuffle.

 Speak with employers and ask which agency they use. Join an agency that is well-respected and used by employers.

5. Head Hunters/Professional Recruiters

    • Similar to placement agencies, but focus on full-time work for professionals.

    • May charge the user a fee, or the employer pays a service fee if they hire you.

    • Different head hunters specialize in different professions.

    • Normally do not offer services or classes such as resume writing.

    • You may register with as many as you like.

    • You must sell yourself and your skills to them so that they can be confident in selling you to employers.

RATINGS:

✓ They often work hard for you, because their salary depends on your success.

✓ They may have access to more contacts than you.

– Some people rely on head hunters as their only job search.

– May be expensive.

"People need responsibility. They resist assuming it, but they cannot get along without it."

—John Steinbeck

6. Professional Resume Services

- The only service they offer is creating your resume.

- Price varies at each location.

- You supply the information, which they format on a computer.

RATINGS:

✓ You **may** be allowed to go back periodically to customize your resume to an extent.

– Your resume may sound impersonal.

– There are no guarantees that you will be satisfied.

– This is the only service offered.

Ask around to find which services people have used. Get as much feedback and information as possible before choosing a service.

Summing It Up

There are many services available for use during your job search. Be sure to look in your area for all those available to you. Take advantage only of those that seem helpful. Remember, these services are not meant to be your only job search strategy. They are meant to be a supplement to your hard work and continuing effort!

Should I Accept The Position?

Have you ever heard people say it is easier to find a job when you already have a job? This is partly due to the fact that you feel more confident when you are employed. Being employed seems to make it easier for you to approach people about where they work, what they do, and if their company is hiring. This raises the question of whether or not you should accept a position you are offered, even if it is not exactly what you want, just so that you are working.

 This may mean it is a contract position or one lower on the corporate ladder than where you think you should be. Maybe the salary is not quite as much as you feel you are worth.

IF:

- the position is related to the field you are seeking employment in

- the company is one you feel comfortable working for

- it is financially feasible

. . . then, yes, accept the position.

WHY?

- If is often easier to network once you are inside a company.

- Sometimes certain positions are only available to internal employees.

- You now have the ability to prove your worth to the company.

- There is no telling what circumstances may change while you are working there: someone may quit, be fired, retire, or a full-time position may become available.

- Contract and/or temporary positions often turn into full-time jobs.

- You now have the entire staff of the company in your network.

"Let him that would move the world, first move himself."

Socrates

Be sure to weigh all options and opportunities carefully before discarding any. You never know where things will lead. The employment market of the future is changing. You will have to be innovative in looking for career and employment opportunities.

Try and focus on today and what you can do, not the past. This means letting go of old attitudes and accepting that the way you look for work may have to change.

It is important that you make things happen in your search instead of waiting for them to happen. By accepting contract, temporary, and entry-level positions, you accept the opportunities and are ready to step through the doors that may open.

Contact Counter

Once you become comfortable with the idea of networking you will be truly amazed at the number of people you are speaking with on a regular basis. It is essential you keep an organized list of all your contacts.

Photocopy the Contact Counter on page 84 as many times as you wish. Fill one out each time you speak to someone new or are given a name to contact. Keep those together in a file and refer to them when planning your day.

You must have an organized system in order to keep track of:

1. Who
   - you spoke to
   - else they referred you to

2. What
   - you spoke about
   - information they require from you—resume, brochure, or business card
   - their company's current hiring needs are

3. Where
   - you will meet them
   - you should send your information and thank-you note

4. Why
   - you should keep in contact with them
   - they are a valuable contact

5. When
   - you will meet with them
   - you should call them again to follow up

6. How
   - you can make sure they remember you
   - you can use the information they provided you with

Remember, you must make the effort to cultivate your contacts. People are often more than willing to help, but they must first see that you are motivated to help yourself.

 "Make new friends, but keep the old; the first are silver the latter, gold."

—Anonymous

```
┌─────────────────────────────────────────────────────────┐
│  𝓒ontact                                                 │
│  𝓒ounter                                                 │
│                                                          │
│  Date: _____                           │
│                                                          │
│  Company Name: _____  │
│                                                          │
│  Contact Name: _____ Title:_____   │
│                                                          │
│  Phone #: _____ │
│                                                          │
│  Appointment Scheduled: ☐ yes  Date/Time: _____ ☐ no │
│                                                          │
│  Follow-up Date: _____                     │
│                                                          │
│  Thank You Mailed: ☐ yes    ☐ no                         │
│                                                          │
│  Resume Submitted  ☐ yes    ☐ no                         │
│                                                          │
│  Comments: _____         │
│  _____ ┌───────┐ │
│  _____ │𝓒ontact│ │
│  _____ │𝓒ounter│ │
│                                                └───────┘ │
└─────────────────────────────────────────────────────────┘
```

Keeping The Momentum

Staying positive and sticking to your job search can be difficult, but you can do it. There are a few things you need to remember.

- Finding a job can be challenging and time-consuming. When you apply for jobs and either hear nothing or receive one of those awful rejection letters, try not to take it personally. Employers are not trying to squash your ego, but are merely informing you that someone else was chosen for the position.

- Read your resume each day. Not only will it prepare you to speak with employers, it will also remind you of what you have to offer and what a valuable person you are.

Organize a pot luck dinner with friends. It costs little and will provide you with positive conversation.

- At the end of each week, review your calendar and see how many contacts you made. Chances are that, along with valuable contacts, you have also made a few friends.

- Keep talking to people. The next person you meet may be your next employer.

- Take time to do things for yourself. You will project a positive image if you feel good.

If you have a bad day, take an idea from a Blues Buster and do something for yourself. You will be amazed at how your outlook changes when you have done something fun. There is no sense in meeting with employers if you can't even smile at yourself in the mirror. You will definitely not make a good impression.

"One must not lose desires. They are mighty stimulants to creativeness, to love, and to long life."

—Alexander A. Bogomoletz

You can do it. Just keep telling yourself that you will succeed. You will get a job soon. Persist and your efforts will pay off.

That Was Then...

- Unemployed meant unproductive.

- Volunteer work was for people who were bored with their days and did not need to work.

- You never approached an employer other than to submit an application or have an interview.

- You never told anyone you were unemployed.

- There were more jobs than people looking.

- Once you found a job you stayed with it until you received your gold watch and pension.

- You only spoke with employers if they were advertising a position.

- If you lost your job, it was your fault.

- You never accepted a job unless it was full-time and permanent.

- You moved because you liked the climate somewhere else, not because of the job situation.

- "Call me next month" meant we don't need your services.

- You checked the career section of the newspaper in the morning, sent out resumes for the jobs you were interested in, and then did something else for the rest of the day.

This Is Now...

- You realize that being unemployed is an economic trend and that you must tell everyone in order to expand your network.

- You toot your own horn, and loudly!

- You speak with employers even if they are not advertising positions.

- Positions are often filled through word of mouth rather than through advertisements.

- You carry and hand out business cards outlining your skills and preferred line of work.

- You use agencies and programs to help you locate employment.

- "Call me next month" means Call me next month!

- You may have as many as five to eight careers in your lifetime.

- Volunteer work is one of the best ways to locate employment.

- Most companies hire part-time or temporary staff.

- You join organizations where you meet people who are in your line of work.

- It often takes several months to secure employment.

- Having one interview for every ten resume submissions is excellent.

Conclusion

You now have the tools, knowledge, and skills necessary for a successful job hunt. The only thing left to do is get started. Who knows? Once you realize how much fun it is meeting new people you may even begin to enjoy the process.

Getting out is the key to meeting people, and meeting people is the key to a successful job hunt. Become a social butterfly and get to know as many people as you possibly can. Eventually, you will meet the person who will be your next employer.

"Whatever you assume to be true will become real for you."

—Dr. Robert Anthony

You are the key to your success. Remember, keep telling yourself you can do it...and you will!